Tracts for the People. No. 4.

WOMAN'S RIGHTS.

BY

REV. JOHN TODD, D.D.,

AUTHOR OF "SERPENTS IN THE DOVES' NEST."

BOSTON:
LEE AND SHEPARD.
1867.

WOMAN'S RIGHTS.

BY

REV. JOHN TODD, D. D.,

AUTHOR OF "SERPENTS IN THE DOVES' NEST."

BOSTON:
LEE AND SHEPARD.
1867.

*Stereotyped at the Boston Stereotype Foundry,
4 Spring Lane.*

PREFACE.

SOUND, as it goes from the bell in the church tower, probably goes in waves and curves, and not in straight lines. Human feeling and thought seem to move in tidal waves, modified, doubtless, by the peculiarities of the age. At one time the women of Rome became so discouraged and down-hearted with their condition, that they committed suicide to such an extent that the Senate, alarmed, passed a decree that all who should henceforth commit suicide should have their bodies exposed, *naked*, in the streets. The instincts of modesty came to woman's aid, and there were no more suicides. On the true instincts of the sex I rely, while I speak to the women of my generation kindly, faithfully, plainly, calmly, and decidedly.

INTRODUCTION.

THE tendency of our generation to break up old associations, and to be emancipated from the beliefs of our fathers, is so strong that many would rather feel relieved to have you convince them that they sprang from a race of apes and gorillas. This is among the male sex. Among the other sex, there is a wide-spread uneasiness, — a discontentment with woman's lot, impatient of its burdens, rebellious against its sufferings, an undefined hope of emancipation from the ordinary lot of humanity by some great revolution, so that her condition will be entirely changed! This feeling crops out in publicly ridiculing marriage, dwelling on its evils, raving about the tyranny of men, crying for the "emancipation of woman," getting up Women's Conventions, and propagating theories, weak, foolish, and criminal. The demand is that we shall acknowledge our abominable cruelty exercised towards woman since her first creation; — that she shall be allowed hereafter to be in all respects equal to man, — shall be educated as he is, enter the same pursuits that he does, receive the same wages, — occupy the same posts and professions, — wield the same influence, and, in a word, be independent of man, — far more independent of him than he ever was or can be of woman. This undefined feeling is not confined to the strong-minded women, who clamor and disgust their sex and ours in demanding "women's rights." It is felt more or less by those who shrink from these moral Camillas.* It is to this class of the sisterhood I am wishing to address myself at this time. Will you allow me then to come and sit down by your side, making no claim to superiority, but sincerely wishing to aid you in coming to most important conclusions?

* "Hos super advenit Volscâ de gente Camilla,
Agmen agens equitum."

WOMAN'S RIGHTS.

EQUALITY OF THE SEXES.

ON this question I shall waste no words. Nobody pretends that the sexes are equal in weight, in height, or in bodily strength. The bodies of the two sexes seem to have been planned for different ends. As to the *mind*, I have no difficulty in admitting that the mind of woman is equal to ours, — nay, if you please, superior. It is quicker, more flexible, more elastic. I certainly have never seen boys learn languages or mathematics, up to a certain point, as fast or as easy as some girls. Woman's intuitions also are far better than ours. She reads character quicker, comes to conclusions quicker, and if I must make a decision on the moment, I had much rather have the woman's decision than man's. She has intuitions given her for her own protection which we have not. She has a delicacy of taste to which we can lay no claim. "Why, then," my lady reader will say, "*why can't we be independent of man?*" for this is the gist of the whole subject. I reply, you can't, for two reasons; first, God never designed you should, and secondly, your own deep instincts are in the way. God never designed that woman should occupy the same sphere as man, because he has given her *a physical organization* so refined and delicate that it can never bear the strain which comes upon the rougher, coarser nature of man. He has hedged her in by laws which no desires or efforts can alter. We, sons of dust, move slower; we creep, where you bound to the head of the stairs at a single leap. And now bear with me, and keep good-natured, while I show you, what you, dear ladies, cannot do, and God don't ask you to do.

1. You cannot invent. There are all manner of inventions in our age, steam, railroads, tele-

graphing, machinery of all kinds, often five hundred and fifty weekly applications for patents at the Patent Office, but among them all no female applicants. You have sewing machines almost numberless, knitting machines, washing, ironing, and churning machines — but I never heard of one that was the emanation of the female mind. Did you? Why sew, or wash, or card off your fingers, rather than to invent, if this was your gift? The old spinning-wheel and the old carding apparatus have gone by, but not by woman's invention. I suppose this power was denied you, lest it should take you out of your most important sphere — as I shall show.

2. You cannot compete with men in a long course of mental labor. Your delicate organization never has and never can bear the study by which you can become Newtons, La Places, or Bowditches in mathematics or astronomy. The world never has seen, and never expects to see, woman excelling in architecture. Neither in ancient or modern times has she one monument of this kind, showing mastership. You

do not find them in ancient Corinth, old Athens, great Rome, or in any city of the old or new world.

So of painting and sculpture. You need not tell us what you are hereafter to do; but you have never yet shown a Phidias, a Raphael, a Michael Angelo, or a Canova. You cannot point to a woman who can pretend to stand by the side of Homer, Virgil, Shakspeare, or Milton. The world has never seen a female historian who came near the first rank. And even in cooking and in millinery, as is well known, men must and do stand at the head of these occupations.

But, you will perhaps say, "we have never had a fair chance — a fair fight in the field. We have been held down by prejudice, and tyranny, and public opinion against us, and all that." Suppose it be so, fair one, there is *one* field you have had to yourself, and nobody has lifted against you one finger. I mean that, for the last half century, we, cruel men, have invented, manufactured, and bought, and brought home, the *piano*, and you have had it all to yourselves.

What is the result? It is, that the master performers, and teachers, and musicians, are men, — is it not? Nay, have you never seen the girl thumping and drumming her piano for years, under the best teachers, and yet her brother come along and take it up, and without any teaching, soon go in advance of the sister? I have seen it often. In none of these departments can woman compete with man. Not because her immortal mind is inferior, — far from it, — but because her bodily organization cannot endure the pressure of continued and long labor as we can. We may deny this, and declare it is not so; but the history of our race, and the state of the world now, show that it is so. I don't say that here and there a woman can't endure much and long; but they are rare exceptions. Did you ever know a woman who could endure being a teacher till seventy-five, as men often do? The fact that in medical colleges, in medical books, in medical practice, woman is recognized as having a peculiar organization, requiring the most careful and gentle treatment, and the consent of the world, all go to show that her bodily powers are not able to endure like those of the other sex. The wheels and workmanship are too delicate to be driven with the mainspring of the old-fashioned bull's-eye. If what I have said seems to want gallantry, I reply, it is not gallantry that I am now after, but facts — truth — the true sphere and power and glory of woman. Be patient. I have some nice and pretty things to say, some garlands to weave, after I have led you to see the great facts of your being. As to "women's rights," I hold that they have great, inalienable, and precious rights, and which I will point out and defend. But he is a poor dog that barks up the wrong tree, however loud or earnest he may bark.

WOMAN'S SPHERE.

The design of God in creating woman was to complete man — a one-sided being without her. Together they make a complete, perfect unit. She has a mission — no higher one could be given her — to be the mother, and *the former of all the character of the human race.* For the first, most important earthly period of life, the race is committed to her, for about twelve years, almost entirely. The human family is what she makes them. She is the queen of the home, its centre, its light and glory. The home, the home is the fountain of all that is good on earth. If she desires a higher, loftier, nobler trust than this, I know not where she can find it. Mother, wife, daughter, sister, are the tenderest, most endearing words in language. Our mothers train us, and we owe everything to them. Our wives perfect all that is good in us, and no man is ashamed to say he is indebted to his wife for his happiness, his influence, and his character, if there is anything noble about him. Woman is the highest, holiest, most precious gift to man. Her mission and throne is the family, and if anything is withheld that would make her more efficient, useful, or happy in that sphere, she is wronged, and has not her "rights."

WHAT HER "RIGHTS" ARE.

If woman steps out of her sphere, and demands to be and to do what men do, to enter political life, to enter the professions, to wrestle with us for office and employments and gains, she must understand that she will have to take the low places as well as the high places of life. She will not be allowed to be a man and be treated with the tenderness due to women. If she goes to Congress, she must also go to the heavy drudgery of earth.

I claim then for her, that it is her "right" to be treated with the utmost love, respect, honor, and consideration in her sphere. I claim that it is her "right" to have every possible aid and advantage to fulfil her mission. I claim that she has a "right" to be let alone there, and not be teased, or flattered, or wheedled out of her place, and made to believe what can never be.

She has a "right" then to be exempted from certain things which men must endure. It is her privilege and her right. She ought to be exempted from the hard drudgery of earth. She ought not to be made a sailor, to hang on the yard-arms, — to chase and kill and try up whales, — to be a surgeon, to pull teeth, cut off legs, or cut out tumors, — to go into the mines, and dig ore and coal, — to burn over the smelting-furnace. She ought not to be compelled to be a barber, a boot-black, to carry hods of brick and mortar up the ladder, — to be a soap boiler, to groom horses, dig canals, dig out peat, tan leather, and stir the tan vats, — to make coffins and dig graves, — to go to the Arctic Ocean for seals, or to spend the long winter in the forest cutting down timber, and in the snow-water of spring to drive logs for hundreds of miles to get these logs out of their native forests. She ought not to be made to butcher, bleed calves, knock down oxen, stick swine, and slaughter cattle. Now she must go in for all this if she leaves her sphere and tries to be a man. I claim that she has a "right" to be exempted. But you may ask, Has she not a *natural* right to enter any and all employments as well as men? Suppose we allow it, and admit that she has a *natural* right to wear jack-boots and spurs, horse-pistols and a sword, and be a complete soldier, and a "natural" right to sing bass and beat a bass-drum, and that *men* have a "natural" right to wear petticoats, dress with low necks, short sleeves, wear pink slippers with paper soles, — but, would it be wise to do so? Dear sisters, you *can't* be good wives, mothers, and crowns of your families, and go into these things — can you?

DRESS.

Some have tried to become semi-men by putting on the Bloomer dress. Let me tell you in a word why it can never be done. It is this: woman, robed and folded in her long dress, is beautiful. She walks gracefully. The very waving of her robes makes the walk graceful. If she attempts to *run*, the charm is gone. Even Venus never tried to run. *Et vera incessu patuit Dea.* So long as she is thus clothed, there is just enough of mystery about woman to challenge admiration, and almost reverence.

Take off the robes, and put on pants and show the limbs, and grace and mystery are all gone. And yet, to be like a man, you must doff your own dress and put on ours. In doing it, you lose more than I can tell. No! Ladies want our respect, and admiration, and reverence too much ever to lay aside their appropriate dress. Their very instincts make them safe here.

VOTING.

A great hue and cry is set up about the right of women to vote, and the cruelty of denying them this right. Plainly this is merely a civil and not a natural right. Minors, foreigners, and idiots are denied it. The property of the world, for the most part, is, and ever has been, and must be, earned by men. It is useful only to support and educate families — our own, or those of others. It would seem best, then, for those who, at any hazard or labor, earn the property. to select the rulers, and have this responsibility The wealth of the age is expended by woman — earned by the man — for the most part. He wants rulers in reference to the industry and business of his age. Let him select them. Moreover, there is something so unseemly in having woman wading in the dirty waters of politics, draggling and wrangling around the ballot-boxes, *e. g.*, mingling with the mobs and rowdies in New York city, that I wonder she ever thinks of it. But "she is a widow, and has property, and pays taxes, — why not vote?" Being a widow, or fatherless, is a misfortune. But the husband or father earned the property, and voted as long as he lived. It may be a misfortune that the property does not now vote, but not so great a misfortune to the world as to have the sex go out of their sphere and enter into political life. Indeed, it is allowed that voting is only the stepping-stone to civil office. But it is stepping out of her sphere, and the moment you do that, you put a few of the sex into office, but depress and degrade at least a thousand where you elevate one. If a few go up, the many go down.

WAGES.

There is great complaint made because justice is not done in compensating labor. It is a hard problem to solve to do this. I know a most excellent pastor, with a noble head and heart, second to few in this commonwealth, who receives only four hundred dollars salary — less than he would have to pay a raw Irish laborer who boarded himself. I know of many receiving five or six hundred dollars. We can't have justice in these matters. But bear in mind that God has put the labor and the duty on men to support the families — wives and children. The man is recreant and guilty if he does not do that; and to do it, and bear the responsibility, he must receive wages accordingly. Is it then so very unjust that woman, who has no such responsibility, does not receive so high wages? You blame employers, and demand that they give females more — a vain demand so long as there are thousands ready to underbid them and do the work cheaper. The demand will pay in proportion to the supply, and no legislation or human power can alter this. Woman can't endure such heavy toil; she can't toil as many hours year after year; she expects to continue the employment but a short time; and the result is, she has to take for her labor the market price for that commodity. But there is a wonderful reason for this great supply, at our day, to which I will allude.

ABNORMITY OF THE COUNTRY.

It must be plain to the thinker that our country and generation are abnormal. That when there are over seventy thousand more females in Massachusetts than there are males, — and probably twice this number in the State of New York, — it is an unnatural condition of things. At the West, through most of the states, the number of men greatly preponderates. Our young men go off early in life, leaving homes, mothers, and sisters behind them. The prospect for these sisters to marry, then, is lessened by every such emigration. Now the question comes, What shall be done in behalf of these thousands of virtuous, educated, and noble girls? The cry is, "Make them into clerks, book-keepers, bankers, and give them all the employments of men. Open all the avenues to employment."

Let us think it over a moment. We are sorry for this state of things, and wish we could remedy it. It is the result of the state of our country, our immense territory, and of our enterprise. But suppose now we make these girls into clerks in stores, in the counting-room, in the insurance office, in the bank, — say ten thousand in Massachusetts and twenty thousand in New York, — don't we displace just so many young men; drive them off to the West; prevent so many new families from being established here; take away thirty thousand chances of marriage from these females, and enhance the evil we are trying to remedy? Is it a blessing to women to lessen her opportunities for marriage? This state of things will eventually right itself, but it bears hard upon women now; but to displace men, to increase the evil, to plan for a present exigency by upturning all the arrangements of Providence, is not wise. We must look at the grand total of results. It is *not* that we wish to keep women from enjoying anything and everything that is for the best good of her sex. I speak of displacing men, and forcing them away. I might add, that from the very instincts of the human heart every public employment diminishes woman's chance of marriage, and in proportion to its publicity.

WOMAN'S EDUCATION.

I lately took up a religious paper, in which no less than *six* "Female Colleges" were advertised and puffed. And we are getting our legislatures to charter new "Female Colleges," and we are boasting how we are about to introduce all the studies and the curriculum of the colleges for men, and we are to put our daughters through them, and educate just as we do men. The thing can never be done. For forty years I have been connected with female seminaries, and have carefully watched their training and results. I say deliberately, that the female has mind enough, talent enough, to go through a complete college course, but her physical organization, as a general thing, will never admit of it. I think the great danger of our day is forcing the intellect of woman beyond what her physical organization will possibly bear. We want to put our daughters at school at six, and have their education completed at eighteen. A girl would feel mortified not to be through schooling by the time she reaches that age. In these years the poor thing has her brain crowded with history, grammar, arithmetic, geography, natural history, chemistry, physiology, botany, astronomy, rhetoric, natural and moral philosophy, metaphysics, French, often German, Latin, perhaps Greek, reading, spelling, committing poetry, writing compositions, drawing, painting, &c., *ad infinitum*. Then out of school hours, from three to six hours of severe toil at the piano. She must be on the strain all the school hours, study in the evening till her eyes ache, her brain whirls, her spine yields and gives way, and she comes through the process of education enervated, feeble, without courage or vigor, elasticity or strength. After a single summer's exhausting study, let sickness strike such a school, and they sink and die most fearfully. Do those who are so strenuous to educate ladies as long and as severely as men *must* be educated for their sphere, know what mortality awaits so many after they are educated? I wish they would examine this point. "Languid and nervous, easily dispirited, instead of feeling within themselves the freshness and buoyancy of youth, what wonder that they draw back, appalled, from their new responsibilities" at marriage. So says a lady writing to me from Minnesota. My unknown correspondent adds, "I have often wished for the tongue of an angel, or a pen of fire, that I might arouse parents, teachers, and school committees to a sense of the wrong they are inflicting on this generation and those to come. I glory in the opportunities for culture of American women, but I pray do not abuse them. Let the girls have time to *grow* as well as to study. If they are not finished scholars at eighteen, what matters it, if they are healthy in body and mind? The mania is a spreading one. Here even in

Minnesota I see it." Alas! must we crowd education upon our daughters, and for the sake of having them "intellectual," make them puny, nervous, and their whole earthly existence a struggle between life and death? If it ministers to vanity to call a girl's school "a college," it is very harmless; but as for training young ladies through a long intellectual course, as we do young men, it can never be done — they will die in the process. Give woman all the advantages and all the education which her organization, so tender and delicate, will bear; but don't try to make the anemone into an oak, nor to turn the dove out to wrestle with storms and winds, under the idea that she may just as well be an eagle as a dove. We Americans belong to the Over-do family. We want to fish the brook dry if we fish at all. We mount hobbies easily because we are "spry;" and now that we have taken woman in hand, we are in danger of educating her into the grave; taking her out of her own beautiful, honored sphere, and making her an hermaphrodite, instead of what God made her to be.

The root of the great error of our day is, that *woman is to be made independent and self-supporting* — precisely what she never can be, because God never designed she should be. Her support, her dignity, her beauty, her honor, and happiness lie in her dependence as wife, mother, and daughter. Any other theory is rebellion against God's law of the sexes, against marriage, which it assails in its fundamental principles, and against the family organization, the holiest thing that is left from Eden.

O woman! your worst enemy is he who scouts at marriage; who tries to flatter you with honeyed words about your rights, while he sneers in his own circle, boasting that "it is cheaper to buy milk than to keep a cow;" who would cruelly lift you out of your sphere, and try to reverse the very laws of God; who tries to make you believe that you will find independence, wealth, and renown in man's sphere, when your only safety and happiness is in patiently, lovingly, and faithfully performing the duties and enacting the relations of your own sphere.

Women of my country! beloved and honored in your own sphere, can't you see that man, rough, stern, cold, almost nerveless, was made to be the *head* of human society; and woman, patient, quick, sensitive, loving, and gentle, is the *heart* of the world? where she may rule and move the world to an extent second to no human power, and where she becomes a blessing greater than we can ever acknowledge, because it is greater than we can measure!

I have spoken to you, gentle ones, kindly and faithfully. Very likely I may have a torrent of abuse poured upon me for it; but it is time that your real friends should no longer have utterance choked. I have tried to select smooth stones from the brook for my sling, and not to wound those whom I would defend; and having said this, I only add, that no provocation will force me to speak on this subject again.

www.ingramcontent.com/pod-product-compliance
Lightning Source LLC
LaVergne TN
LVHW011123110826
845150LV00008B/2238

* 9 7 8 1 4 1 8 1 9 5 4 0 3 *